# WE BOTH READ®

## Parent's Introduction

We Both Read is the first series of books designed to invite parents and children to share the reading of a story by taking turns reading aloud. This "shared reading" innovation, which was developed with reading education specialists, invites parents to read the more complex text and storyline on the left-hand pages. Then, children can be encouraged to read the right-hand pages, which feature less complex text and storyline, specifically written for the beginning reader.

Reading aloud is one of the most important activities parents can share with their child to assist them in their reading development. However, We Both Read goes beyond reading *to* a child and allows parents to share the reading *with* a child. We Both Read is so powerful and effective because it combines two key elements in learning: "modeling" (the parent reads) and "doing" (the child reads). The result is not only faster reading development for the child, but a much more enjoyable and enriching experience for both!

You may find it helpful to read the entire book aloud yourself the first time, then invite your child to participate in the second reading. In some books, a few more difficult words will first be introduced in the parent's text, distinguished with **bold lettering**. Pointing out, and even discussing, these words will help familiarize your child with them and help to build your child's vocabulary. Also, note that a "talking parent" icon ⌖ precedes the parent's text and a "talking child" icon ⌖ precedes the child's text.

We encourage you to share and interact with your child as you read the book together. If your child is having difficulty, you might want to mention a few things to help him. "Sounding out" is good, but it will not work with all words. Children can pick up clues about the words they are reading from the story, the context of the sentence, or even the pictures. Some stories have rhyming patterns that might help. It might also help them to touch the words with their finger as they read, to better connect the voice sound and the printed word.

Sharing the We Both Read books together will engage you and your child in an interactive adventure in reading! It is a fun and easy way to encourage and help your child to read—and a wonderful way to start them off on a lifetime of reading enjoyment!

# About Dogs
We Both Read® Book

---

Text Copyright © 2009 by Treasure Bay, Inc.
Use of photographs provided by Fotosearch and Getty Images.
All rights reserved

We Both Read® is a trademark of Treasure Bay, Inc.

Published by
Treasure Bay, Inc.
P.O. Box 119
Novato, CA 94948 USA

Printed in Singapore

Library of Congress Control Number:  2009924401

Hardcover ISBN-13:  978-1-60115-237-4
Paperback ISBN-13:  978-1-60115-238-1

We Both Read® Books
Patent No. 5,957,693

Visit us online at:
www.webothread.com

PR 07/10

# About Dogs

By Bruce Johnson and Sindy McKay

TREASURE BAY

*Jack Russell terrier puppy*

Do you have a dog? Do you know someone who has a dog? There are millions of dogs in the world, so you probably know at least . . .

 . . . one dog.

*Beagle puppies*

 Why are dogs so popular?

It might be because they are smart, helpful, and playful. They make wonderful . . .

 . . . pets.

 The size and shape of dogs usually depend on their breed. Each breed is a different kind of dog. The dogs in a breed all share similar characteristics, including the way they look. **Some** breeds, like Yorkshire terriers, are short. **Some**, like dachshunds, are long. **Some** breeds are small.

 **Some** are big.

Certain breeds have long **hair**, like the chow chow or komondor. Other breeds have short **hair**, like the beagle or boxer. One breed has almost . . .

. . . no **hair!**

 A purebred dog may be entered in a dog **show**. Here, he competes against other dogs to demonstrate that he is the best example of his breed.

The highest honor a dog can win at a dog **show** is called . . .

 . . ."Best in **Show**."

*Border collie*

Both purebreds and mixed-breed dogs can make great family pets. Good family dogs are friendly and active. **They like** kids.

**They like** to play.

*Gray wolf*

Why are there so many different kinds of dogs?

Long ago, most dogs looked like wolves. Some of these wolf-dogs were **smarter** and had better skills at hunting, herding, or guarding. People bred the dogs to bring out these skills.

*Yellow Labrador retriever*

 Dogs are **smart!**

Many years ago, people hunted for much of their food. There weren't any grocery stores back then. A dog that could help capture or retrieve prey was a big help.

Many breeds of hunting dogs are still used by sport hunters today.

Run, run, run!

 Sled dogs were bred by the peoples of the polar regions. These dogs could pull heavy loads and haul food to villages.

Today, they are sometimes used in sled-dog races.

 Good dogs!

Different types of herding dogs have been trained to herd cattle, **sheep**, goats, and even reindeer. They keep the flock together and guard them from predators and thieves.

 Stop, **sheep!**

*German shepherd*

⊙ Search-and-rescue dogs are hard-working heroes. They find people who are trapped or lost by **sniffing** with their sensitive noses.

Sniff, sniff.

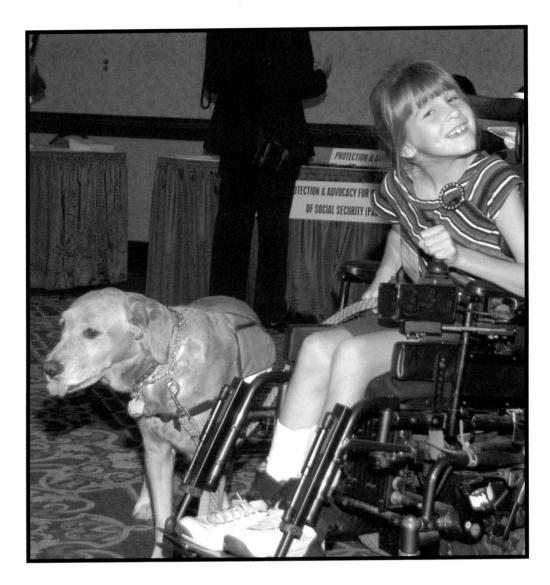

Assistance dogs **help** people with disabilities. Hearing dogs **help** the deaf by alerting them to sounds. Service dogs might **help** people in wheelchairs to retrieve objects that are out of reach. Guide dogs act as eyes for the blind.

 Dogs can **help.**

Being smart and helpful are not the only reasons we love dogs. We also love them because they make such good companions. A dog can be your best friend.

 Dogs are fun!

 If you have a dog, you know it takes work to care for her. She must always have plenty of fresh water, have good food to **eat**, and should see a veterinarian at least once a year.

Dogs **eat** a lot.

*Golden retriever*

Most dogs also need lots of exercise. People often take their dogs for walks, but some dogs need to . . .

 . . . run and jump!

Agility courses are another wonderful way for your dog to get exercise. He can jump over, leap through, and run around various obstacles. But the best way just might be to go in your backyard and have fun!

#  Play ball!

 Some owners take their dogs to "dog school." Professional trainers can teach dogs to sit, stay, fetch, and come when you call them.

Sit up!

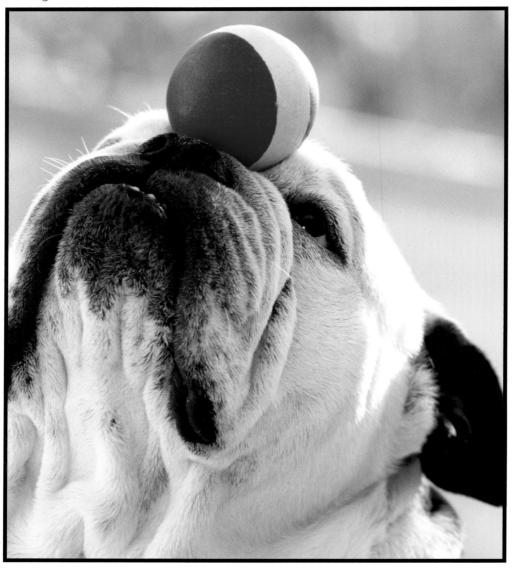

Dogs can also learn to do funny tricks, like barking on cue or balancing a ball on their nose. You might even be able to teach your dog to count. This dog can count . . .

 . . . to ten.

There are many reasons why dogs make great pets. If you treat them well, they will be with you for a long, long time— a friend to . . .

 . . . the end.

# Fun Facts about Dogs

- The Basenji is the only barkless dog in the world.

- Greyhounds can reach speeds up to 45 miles per hour.

- The most popular breed of dog in the United States is the Labrador retriever.

- The oldest known dog lived to be 29 years and 5 months old.

- The highest jump by a dog was 68 inches. This is almost 6 feet.

Parents,

Here are three questions about dogs to ask your child. Let the answers spark discussion.

1. Think about some dogs you know. Would you say they are big or small? Have long hair or short hair? How else could you describe them?

2. Name three ways dogs can help people.

3. What are some things that must be done to take good care of a dog?

If you liked **About Dogs**, here is another
We Both Read® book you are sure to enjoy!

## We All Sleep

This nonfiction book for very beginning readers
uses a touch of humor as it shows how different
animals sleep. From pigs to puppies to penguins,
the book offers glimpses of animals as they live,
play, and sleep. In the end, the book even has the
readers talking about falling asleep themselves!
Rhymes and repeating text help make the reading
fun and easy for the child.